I0189251

IMAGES
of America

OAKLAND
POLICE DEPARTMENT

ON THE COVER: This photograph shows the Oakland Police Department (OPD) Motorcycle Drill Team at a Veterans Day Parade in 1954. (Courtesy of the Oakland Public Library.)

IMAGES
of America

OAKLAND
POLICE DEPARTMENT

Phil McArdle

ARCADIA
PUBLISHING

Copyright © 2007 by Phil McArdle
ISBN 978-1-5316-2885-7

Published by Arcadia Publishing
Charleston SC, Chicago IL, Portsmouth NH, San Francisco CA

Library of Congress Catalog Card Number: 2006938516

For all general information contact Arcadia Publishing at:
Telephone 843-853-2070
Fax 843-853-0044
E-mail sales@arcadiapublishing.com
For customer service and orders:
Toll-Free 1-888-313-2665

Visit us on the Internet at www.arcadiapublishing.com

In memory of Officer Roger Wallace and Officer Mike Soto

"I subscribe firmly to the belief that all of us, in whatever endeavor, owe much to those who preceded us and that we must look back—at least occasionally—to ensure that we are benefiting from the wisdom of the past."

—George T. Hart
Chief of Police, 1973–1994
(Letter to the author, April 1995)

CONTENTS

ACKNOWLEDGMENTS

I could not have written a history of the Oakland Police Department for the general public without the generous assistance of its members and employees, past and present. Though I cannot list everyone who helped, I am especially indebted to Capt. James MacArthur and to Officer Ron Gunnar, then president of the Oakland Police Officers Association, who got me interested in this subject one bright morning many years ago. Little did they know what they had started!

I owe thanks to the following members and employees of the department, past and present, living and dead, for their friendship and unfailing help: Chiefs George Hart, Lester Divine, Joseph Samuels, Richard Word, and Wayne Tucker; Deputy Chiefs Bradley Kearns and William H. Brock; Capts. Bob Ford, Thorvald "Ted" Brown, John Giudici, and Michael Meyers; Lieutenants Harold Mijanovich and Dave Downing; Inspectors John Connolly, James Mangini, and Roderick Petersen; Sgt. Dexter Mast; Officers Tom Campbell, Chuck Teich, and Tim Sanchez; criminalist Mary Gibbons; senior dispatchers Phyllis Bruening and Virginia Tomek; Frank Alliger, Records Division; and Scarlet Ku and Lynn Freedman, Planning Division.

Outside the department I could not have done without the expert help of people who took the time to answer my questions or to help me find a photograph: Bill Sturm, Larry Odoms, Don Hausler, and Steve Levoy (Oakland Public Library); Sibylle Zemitis (California State Library, Sacramento); Augie Sairanen (*San Francisco Chronicle*); Gareth Mast; and Dr. Peter Conmy (Oakland city historian). Mark Hutchins of the Alameda County District Attorney's Office generously allowed me to quote from *Point of View*. I am also, of course, indebted to my friend Robert Middleton, who worked at the police department and at the Port of Oakland and who kindly reviewed the text of this book. Collectively, they saved me from hundreds of mistakes. Any surviving errors in this work are my responsibility. Unless otherwise noted, all photographs are courtesy of the Oakland Police Department or the author.

As always, I owe thanks to my wife, Karen, for her help.

INTRODUCTION

The story of the Oakland Police Department covers a period of more than 150 years. It tells how an agency that began in a dusty small town during the Gold Rush became a modern police enforcement department in an important American city. Beginning with only three members, today it is a large, complex, multifaceted organization with more than a 1,000 officers and employees. The department and the city it serves grew side-by-side.

Before Oakland came to be, the land on which it stands was inhabited for several thousand years by a Native American people commonly known as the Ohlones. In 1820, it became part of Rancho San Antonio, a Spanish land grant of 45,000 acres, which stretched from San Leandro in the south to Albany in the north, and from the shores of San Francisco Bay east to the tops of the Contra Costa hills. The Spanish way of life was overwhelmed by events following the Mexican-American War and the discovery of gold at Sutter's Mill.

In 1849, Harry Morse, a future sheriff of Alameda County, arrived in California as a crewman on an East India packet. Fifty years later, he wrote down his first impressions of the East Bay:

> There was something strangely attractive to the ship's crew in the long, low sweep of coast on the shore opposite San Francisco. The vivid green of the live oaks looked in the dim distance like an oasis in the midst of a great, brown countryside. The low shoreline was backed up by high hills, upon some of whose ridges grew immense redwood trees. The crew's curiosity about the "Contra Costa" grew, and finally a few of us determined on an exploring expedition. Obtaining one of the ship's small boats we set sail on the fair morning of August 5, 1849, and landed at about the foot of Oakland's present Broadway. That is how I came to see the oak groves and the site of the city in all of its untouched, original beauty. Oakland was then a grand park of "encinas," or live oak trees, with an underbrush of wild blackberry bushes. We walked up from the waterfront into the edge of these mighty trees, and gazed about us with a feeling of surprise and pleasure at the beautiful vistas spread before us. There was nothing to break the solitude of the place except the occasional lowing of semi-wild cattle or the bleating of calves belonging to the herd. . . . The undergrowth was full of quail, while now and then a deer would start up and bound away, giving a startled, almost reproachful look at the intruders. The country was lovely, the climate delightful. Here, in the Contra Costa, nature had been most prodigal.

In the 1850s, the police department patrolled a village surrounded by ranch land and farms. When Oakland became the western terminus of the transcontinental railroad in 1869, it began developing as a port and an industrial center. After 1911, heavy industry increased rapidly, including the manufacture of ships and automobiles. Oakland's rapid growth between 1911 and 1929 slowed to a crawl during the Great Depression, picked up again during World War II and the immediate postwar years, slowed again in the 1950s, and began a long recovery in the 1970s.

For Oakland, the 20th century was a time of great opportunity and unprecedented challenges. It was marked by dizzying economic cycles, alternating between deep depression and soaring prosperity; by mass movements of population, internally and externally; by natural disasters—earthquakes and fires; and by dreadful man-made catastrophes—two World Wars and wars in Korea and Vietnam. The people of Oakland were tested by crusades against fascism abroad and racism at home.

These events changed Oakland and its police department in a host of ways, bringing unexpected gains and losses. Halfway through the 20th century, when a national civic organization designated Oakland an "All-American city," the attribution was deeply accurate in ways far beyond the intentions of simple boosterism.

Beginning on a few acres along a boggy estuary, Oakland has grown into a city that covers 60 square miles and has a waterfront 32 miles long. It began the last century as a predominantly European-American community, culturally homogeneous, and in transition from a town into a city. (As chief of police Wilson noted in 1906, "We are rapidly advancing along metropolitan lines.") By 1999, it had become one of the largest cities in California, home to a dynamic multicultural, multiracial population of more than 350,000 people. Its population includes Caucasians, African Americans, Hispanics, Native Americans, and Asians. Oakland is still growing and still changing. Today it sees its future as a center for information technology.

One

FRONTIER DAYS

Not long after Harry Morse visited the Oakland estuary, Americans began settling along the shoreline and moving inland. Some of them bought or leased property from the Peralta family in honest, straightforward transactions. Others—squatters—staked claims on the theory that the Mexican-American War cancelled all Spanish land grants. Claim jumping was common, and in 1849 and 1850, there were shootings over prime pieces of land.

Honest settlers formed vigilance committees for self-protection. In 1852, for example, one committee of ranchers seized two brothers who ran a slaughterhouse near Fourteenth Avenue and East Eighteenth Street and charged them with cattle rustling. There was little reason to doubt they stole cows from ranches in the hills, slaughtered them, and sold the meat in San Francisco. After a quick trial, they were hanged and buried in unmarked graves at the water's edge.

Out of this disorder, one dominating figure emerged: Horace Carpentier, the ambitious lawyer who founded Oakland. He saw the need to organize a competent city government with a police force to provide regular law enforcement. The first officers were appointed in 1853. It took time for them to establish their authority, but day by day they helped to make the town quiet and law-abiding.

In *Municipal Justice in the Melting Pot*, Robert Percival analyzed Oakland's 19th-century arrest records. He found that "at the start of the period, the number of arrests made annually in Oakland was minuscule; only 368 arrests . . . in 1868." The city physician reported only two homicides between 1870 and 1875. The records showed only "197 arrests for felonies against property" in 1875. By 1890, when 66,690 people lived in Oakland, the number of arrests rose to 4,180. "From this peak," Percival states, "The number of arrests declined in seven of the 10 years of the 1890s." In 1900, there were only 35 arrests for property felonies. It appears that Mayor Andrus described the 19th-century reality when he said, in 1879, "Life and property are unusually secure in Oakland." This was a remarkable achievement for the department and, especially, for the people of Oakland.

Ohlone Indians dance at Mission San Jose, c. 1807, in this painting by George Heinrich von Langsdorff. Descendants of these Native Americans still live in the East Bay.

The Peralta land grant encompassed the future city of Oakland and all of Alameda County. The Peraltas were ranchers and lived lightly on the land. The ranch house pictured here, and still standing at Thirty-fourth and Paxton Avenues, is one of the few remaining signs of Rancho San Antonio. Descendants of the original Peraltas live in the East Bay, but they are no longer landholders.

Horace Carpentier (right), Edson Adams, and A. J. Moon each claimed 160 acres of land between First and Fourteenth Streets and Market and Fallon Streets, with Broadway running through the center. Carpentier drafted Oakland's charter and got it approved by the state legislature before very many people in town knew what was afoot. He became the town's first mayor. (Courtesy of the Oakland Public Library.)

Oakland's first town council was elected in 1852 and met in this simple wooden building on Broadway, between Third and Fourth Streets. Oakland's early elections were irregular by today's standards. An 1854 census estimated that 300 people lived in the town. Horace Carpentier was elected to the state legislature that year with 519 votes; his opponents received 254 and 192 votes, respectively. A total of 965 votes were counted, but there were only 130 registered voters in the county.

According to Beth Bagwell's *Oakland: The Story of a City*, this is "the earliest known view of Oakland." It was drawn between 1852 and 1854, by an anonymous artist. The drawing is from the Embarcadero and Broadway, looking east toward the hills. (Courtesy of the Oakland Public Library.)

The rough-and-ready era reached its climax when men described as "a horde of outlaws," and who were ordered out of San Francisco by the vigilance committee, decided to attempt a mass claim jump in Oakland. They crossed the bay by ferry, but news of their plans preceded them. When the ferry approached the Oakland dock, it was met by people in a fighting mood who had equipped themselves with firearms and a cannon. The ferry turned around and headed back to San Francisco. Someone touched off the canon (known ever after as "the old Squatter Gun") to speed them on their way. (Courtesy of the Oakland Public Library.)

J. P. M. Davis was elected marshal of Oakland in 1855. Although he served only one term, he seemed to have acquired a taste for public service and had just been elected mayor in 1860 when this photograph was taken. (Courtesy of the Oakland Public Library.)

This unprepossessing building is said to have housed Oakland's first jail and the police court (the equivalent of today's municipal court). The town council appointed Oakland's first officers on October 15, 1853—John McCann as town marshal and two deputies, R. W. Kellogg and William McCaw. They were paid $150 a month, provided with a budget of $75 for badges, and charged with maintaining public order and collecting taxes. (Courtesy of the Oakland Public Library.)

Built as a toll bridge in 1853 by T. C. Gilman and Horace Carpentier, the Twelfth Street Bridge connected East and West Oakland, making it possible for the first time to travel across the city without taking a long detour around the edges of the San Antonio Slough (today's Lake Merritt). This was important to the ranchers in East Oakland and outlying areas who drove their cattle to market. As the town got larger, herds of cattle became a dangerous annoyance, and a section was added to the municipal code prohibiting "cattle being driven through the streets between the hours of six o'clock a.m. and 12 o'clock midnight." (Courtesy of the Oakland Public Library.)

As a young man, writer Bret Harte rented rooms at Fifth and Clay Streets from 1854 to 1857. Those four years introduced Harte to characters who turned up later in his fiction and gave him the personal experience of Spanish and Mexican life that enriched stories like "The Devotion of Henriquez." These tales—and there are only a few of them—are the sole artistic record of the days when the new town was as likely to be called "The Encinal" as Oakland. Harte's stepfather, Andrew Williams (a political opponent of Horace Carpentier's), served a term as mayor in 1857. (Courtesy of the Oakland Public Library.)

In 1861, the College of California occupied the four square blocks downtown between Twelfth and Fourteenth Streets and Franklin and Harrison Streets. Other institutions of higher learning in 19th-century Oakland included Mills College, the College of Holy Names, and St. Mary's College. (Courtesy of the Oakland Public Library.)

Public transit began with horse-drawn trolleys. When the College of California moved to Berkeley, a special tram line was run up Telegraph Avenue for students and faculty commuting into the barren Berkeley hills. The police also used the trolleys to escort petty offenders to jail. (Courtesy of the Oakland Public Library.)

15

Oakland was strongly pro-Union during the Civil War, and locomotives with patriotic names began to appear on city streets. The "Liberty" was one of the first, running along Seventh Street to a pier where a ferry docked. The pier developed into the Oakland Mole, an artificial harbor built as an anchorage for ferryboats, and the police patrolled it to provide for public safety. On one occasion, when a member of China's royal family made a state visit to the Bay Area, officers intercepted a revolutionary who wanted to assassinate him. (Courtesy of the Oakland Public Library.)

When transcontinental trains began arriving in Oakland in 1869, passengers disembarked at the city's brand new station, conveniently located at Seventh Street and Broadway. Everything needed to make Oakland a great transportation and commercial center was now in place. (Courtesy of the Oakland Public Library.)

16

In October 1867, Richard D. Richardson became the first Oakland police officer to lose his life in the line of duty. A court issued an order for an old man and his wife to be evicted from a house where they were living illegally, and Officer Richardson was directed to serve it. When Richardson came to the door, the old man shot and killed him. Officer Richardson was 35 years old and left a wife and three children.

After the shooting of Officer Richardson, a mob gathered with the intention of lynching the killer. Sheriff Morse, who happened to be in the area, faced down the mob, commandeered a buckboard, and took the killer and his wife to the county jail in San Leandro. The murderer, 70 years old at the time of the shooting, died in jail five days before his trial would have begun. His wife was not charged in the crime, and what became of her is not known. (Courtesy of the Oakland Public Library.)

This tranquil scene was at the corner of Sixth Street and Broadway, looking east, on an ordinary day in 1869. (Courtesy of the Oakland Public Library.)

This photograph shows Mary J. Sanderson (center) and her students at the Brooklyn Colored School in 1870. There were small numbers of African Americans present in Alameda County from the earliest days of the American settlement. The "Special Census—Contra Costa County 1852" (which included the whole East Bay from Concord to Hayward) lists "six black American men, one black American woman, and eight black men from other countries." Eight years later, in 1860, by which time Oakland had a population of 1,543, the federal Census listed seven "colored" people living in Oakland. The establishment of an African American community began with the arrival of the transcontinental railroads. (Courtesy of the Oakland Public Library.)

Here is another tranquil Oakland scene, c. 1870, looking south from Broadway and Twelfth Street. At this time, even though parts of Broadway had been paved, most streets in Oakland were still dirt roads. The College of California can be seen in the background. (Courtesy of the Oakland Public Library.)

This view of the Oakland Mole at the foot of Seventh Street was drawn in 1878. It shows Chinese workers in the foreground with trains and ships behind them. (Courtesy of the Oakland Public Library.)

The Alameda County Courthouse was located at Broadway and Fourth Street from 1872 to 1937. Criminal cases too serious for the police court were tried in this ornate Victorian building. (Courtesy of the Oakland Public Library.)

Walking his beat, the early Oakland policeman was an isolated figure. He could only summon help by blowing his whistle or, in an extreme emergency, shooting his gun in the air. The development of call boxes enabled officers to talk to headquarters directly. By 1886, only 10 years after Alexander Graham Bell invented the telephone, Oakland had installed 39 "police telegraph boxes."

This beautiful building was Oakland's fourth city hall. Located at Fourteenth and Washington Streets, it housed the city administration and the police department. Shortly after this photograph was taken in 1877, it burned to the ground in a terrible fire. The city jail was on the very bottom floor, and Capt. Dave Rand risked his own life to rescue the prisoners. (Courtesy of the Oakland Public Library.)

Captain Rand died less than a year after the fire at city hall. In a memorial proclamation, the city council said of him, "Whatever he did was done well . . . he shirked no duty [and] dared to face danger . . . in every sense . . . he was a true citizen and a bold exponent of the right." (Courtesy of the Oakland History Room.)

In the mid-19th century, Chinatown was in West Oakland, near the foot of Castro Street. Later it moved to its current location, between Franklin and Harrison Streets. Many households relied on Chinese workers for the regular delivery of fresh fish, fruit, and vegetables. (Courtesy of the Oakland Public Library.)

Dennis Holland became one of the department's notable detectives. After he retired in 1920, he told an inquiring reporter this story as an example of the cases he dealt with in the 1880s:

I remember in particular a band of horse and rig thieves that caused us a lot of worry. . . . They used to work on Wednesday and Sunday nights, stealing handsome carriages and good horses from the church folk. They worked in Oakland, San Francisco, Sacramento, Berkeley and Alameda and had their headquarters in San Jose. It took a long time to discover their San Jose headquarters, about two years, in fact, but we finally landed them. They had taken the horses and pastured them out, selling them singly, and had a big plant where they repainted the carriages and fixed them up so their own owners wouldn't know them. (Courtesy of the OPD.)

Trolley lines soon reached into all parts of Oakland. This line gave its name to a part of the city—Trestle Glen.

Captain Wilson on parade.

Adelbert Wilson became one of Oakland's most distinguished officers. During his long career, he was offered the post of captain of police, and later chief of police, several times, but always refused because the job "was in politics" and "a plum which successive administrations plucked for special favorites." When his pension was secure and civil service reform seemed to mean he could not be dismissed out of hand, he accepted the position in 1906. (Courtesy of the OPD.)

W. R. Thomas became captain of police in 1885. This photograph was taken after his election as mayor in 1897. (Courtesy of the Oakland Public Library.)

In 1886, the department purchased the patrol wagon seen here, possibly stopped on Fifteenth Street near today's city hall and Frank Ogawa Plaza, between the State Building and The Rotunda. According to the *Overland Review*, it was the first patrol wagon used west of the Mississippi River, and in emergencies, it doubled as an ambulance. When it was unavailable, officers were authorized "to hire a horse and buggy . . . but in no case shall the cost exceed $10." Years later, Chief Petersen identified the men in the photograph as Officer McKinney and Officer Paul R. Rand, the brother of Capt. Dave Rand. (Courtesy of the Oakland Public Library.)

Known as "Old City Hall," this elegant building was replaced in 1914 by Oakland's current city hall. (Courtesy of the Oakland Public Library.)

Chief Willard F. Fletcher is seated in the center, with Capt. Adelbert Wilson at his right. Chief Fletcher led the department twice, as captain of police in 1887 and, after the job title changed, as chief in 1898. According to the 1916 *History of the Police Department*, he showed "efficiency and capability" in both terms. It also stated, "Captain Fletcher is living and is still hale and hearty. He enjoys that ripe age which comes from an active life and the satisfaction which comes from knowing that he performed all his official duties in a highly honorable manner." (Courtesy of the Oakland Public Library.)

Chief Fletcher is surrounded by members of the department in a photograph taken behind old city hall.

26

On a quiet morning at Seventh and Washington Streets in the 1890s, the Women's Christian Temperance Union coffee room is open for business. (The WCTU, founded in 1874, played an important part in the crusade for prohibition.) At this time, however, Washington Street was a shopping district for the residential areas close to downtown. (Courtesy of the Oakland Public Library.)

Jack London, the author of *White Fang, Call of the Wild,* and other stories, attended the University of California in the 1890s. After dropping out of school, he became a speaker for the Socialist Labor Party. For better or worse, he was arrested on February 10, 1897, by Officer Henderson for violation of OMC 1676, which made it "unlawful for any person to conduct or take part in any public meeting held on any public street situated within the fire limits of the City of Oakland unless permission . . . has first been obtained in writing from the Mayor." He may have been the first protester from Berkeley ever arrested in Oakland.

London spent a lot of time at his friend Johnny Heinhold's First and Last Chance Saloon when he was writing *Tales of the Fish Patrol.* He based these high-spirited stories on his work with the State Fish Patrol, an agency that enforced early environmental laws meant to protect San Francisco Bay from overfishing.

President McKinley visited Oakland and the Bay Area in May 1901 and delivered a speech at a spot on Oak Street beside Lake Merritt. The department provided security for him with mounted officers beside his carriage and sharpshooters deployed throughout the area. President McKinley travelled in fear for his life, and he was assassinated four months after his visit to Oakland.

Idora Park, pictured above, was a resort at Fortieth Street and Telegraph Avenue. With its roller coaster, merry-go-round, and dance floor, it was one of the most popular places in Oakland.

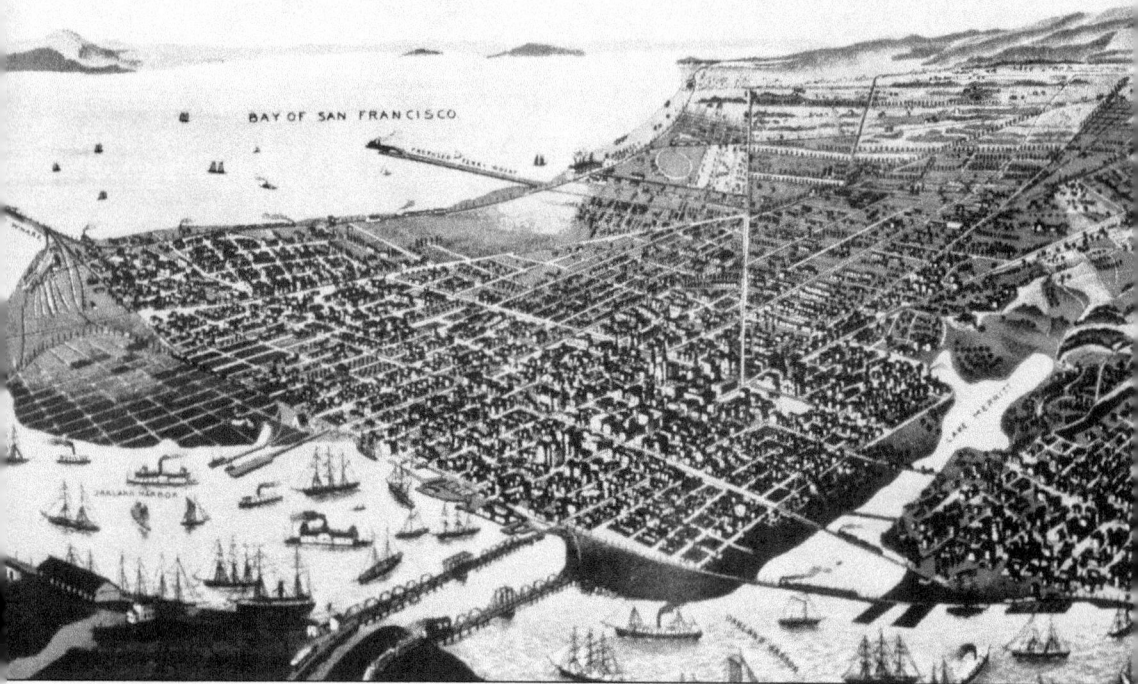

This drawing presents an aerial view of Oakland at the end of the 19th century. Although not to scale, it captures the shape of the city after 50 years of steady growth. By this time, almost 70,000 people lived in Oakland. The city was prosperous by the standards of the time, even though the average wage was 22¢ an hour and annual salaries ranged between $200 and $400. The average citizen had a life expectancy of 47 years and could expect to die of pneumonia or tuberculosis. (Courtesy of the Oakland Public Library.)

Two

THE 1906 EARTHQUAKE

Oakland and Northern California have been struck by three major earthquakes during the past century and a half—in 1868, 1906, and 1989. Seismologists estimate that the 1868 earthquake would have registered 7.0 on the Richter scale. This temblor, which was on the Hayward fault, did relatively little damage and caused few fatalities because the region was so lightly settled. It gave people in Oakland quite a scare, though, and was known for the rest of the century as "The Great San Francisco Earthquake."

At 5:10 a.m. on Wednesday, April 18, 1906, an earthquake with a magnitude of 7.9 ruptured the San Andreas Fault for over 300 miles. From San Juan Bautista in the south to Point Arena in the north, it caused astonishing damage and loss of life. Thousands of people died in San Francisco.

Once again, however, Oakland suffered relatively little. Some buildings were destroyed, and water, telephone, and telegraph services were disrupted briefly. A few people did not even notice it. One man who picked up morning papers at the Oakland Mole for delivery in Berkeley was driving his buckboard along Telegraph Avenue when it hit. "I didn't feel any earthquake in my cart," he said, "But as I came along I wondered why so many people were out on the streets so early, so I stopped at Alcatraz Avenue to find out. They told me there had been a pretty hard earthquake, but that was all they knew."

Mayor Mott and Chief Wilson immediately recognized the quake as a major disaster, and they took decisive measures to deal with it. All of Oakland's police officers were called back to duty for the emergency, and the mayor sent for assistance from the army. The department's performance during the earthquake was the greatest test it had ever faced. In dealing with all of its demands, Chief Wilson and his officers achieved an outstanding success.

That afternoon, as smoke darkened the sky over San Francisco, the first of more than 150,000 refugees arrived, and citizen committees began providing them with food and shelter. When the army arrived, it found the police had kept the city in good order, and the troops were free to expedite the distribution of food and clothing. Oakland's population tripled within a few days, and there was an enormous amount of relief work to be done.

Mayor Frank Mott had been in office less than a year when the earthquake hit. A 10-year veteran of the city council, he was beginning what became a decade as mayor. (Courtesy of the Oakland Public Library.)

When the earthquake struck, Adelbert Wilson, a member of the force for 37 years, had been chief for only two months. (Courtesy of the Oakland Public Library.)

At Twelfth Street and Broadway, the Empire Theater collapsed into the building next door, killing five people. Many other buildings sustained structural damage as well. (Courtesy of the Oakland Public Library.)

The wall on this building (above left) fell away during the earthquake. Thousands of people were helped by police, soldiers, and civilian volunteers at city hall and other relief centers across the city (above right).

A refugee camp was set up at Adams Point (today's Lakeside Park), and this photograph shows some of the orderly rows of tents in which the displaced people lived for a time. People were also given shelter at Idora Park. By year's end, the city appeared to have returned to normal, but it actually was never the same again. Some 65,000 of the refugees decided to stay and live in Oakland, and this population increase—the largest in the city's history—marked the transformation of Oakland from a small town into a big city. (Courtesy of the Oakland Public Library.)

Three

THE PROGRESSIVE ERA

"The city is the storm center of our civilization," wrote Walter J. Petersen, Oakland's chief of police in 1915. In his time, the nation changed from an agricultural to an industrial society. As urban populations increased, institutions throughout the country were subjected to unprecedented stress. The Progressive Movement arose in response, calling for moral, social, and political reforms, and Mayor Frank Mott embodied the spirit of progressive change in Oakland. His efficient leadership during the 1906 earthquake gave him the stature to put through a host of civic improvements. He supported the modernizing efforts of Chief Wilson and Chief Petersen, which transformed the department from a 19th-century police force into a modern one, and constructed the framework of the department known today.

These were years of unprecedented growth. In 1900, Oakland had a population of 67,690 and a police force of 61 officers (71 by the time of the earthquake). By 1920, it had a population of 216,261 residents, and the police force had 250 officers.

In the Progressive Era, the department became the first west of the Mississippi to apply two new developments to policing—automobiles and fingerprints. It began systematic traffic control, modern record keeping, and adopted civil service reforms.

During World War I, many Oakland police officers (including Chief Petersen) joined the armed forces and served overseas. For those who remained at home, the problems of wartime were added to their responsibility for public safety. Patrol of the estuary and other special measures were successful. However, gambling, prostitution, and pre-Prohibition alcohol violations reached such a level that military authorities threatened several times to declare Oakland off limits to soldiers and sailors. During the Spanish influenza pandemic of 1918–1919, Chief Nedderman and volunteers from the department helped Dr. Daniel Crosby, the city physician, set up a desperately needed influenza hospital in the Oakland Auditorium.

The Progressive Era began winding down with the election of Mayor Davie in 1915. It ended in 1919 after the Oakland regiments returned from the war, cheered by huge crowds before they were demobilized.

Mayor Mott (right) welcomes Secretary of State William Jennings Bryant to Oakland. Mott's administration was pointed to as an example of good government in contrast to the machine politics of San Francisco. (Courtesy of the Oakland History Room.)

Adelbert Wilson was chief of police from January 2, 1906, until his retirement on October 1, 1912. He is in the front passenger seat of the department's 1908 Pope-Hartford automobile with, from left to right, Captain Petersen, Captain Lynch, Captain Bock, Sergeant Curtis, and Officer Ahern. Wilson obtained civil service status for police officers in 1911, a reform that was saluted as ending political patronage in the department. (Courtesy of the Oakland History Room.)

The police soon realized the automobile could be more than a nuisance—its speed and mobility made it ideal for patrol in outlying areas. In October 1906, Chief Wilson proposed experimenting with one, and the city council appropriated $250 to rent a 1906 Auto-Car. Its owner drove the rented vehicle "to City Hall with pomp and ceremony each evening at 6 o'clock, to serve as a taxi for the police until 2 a.m. the next morning," making Oakland the first police department west of the Mississippi to use a patrol car. By mid-December, the Auto-Car's success in dispatching officers to crime scenes led the council to authorize the purchase of "a permanent machine." An Auto-Car cost about $3,000 and had a four-cylinder engine. (Courtesy of the Oakland History Room.)

The motorcycle pictured here was probably the department's first. It was used for the traffic enforcement program, which began when Chief Wilson decided to "stop fast driving" by enforcing the 10-mile-per-hour speed limit for horseless carriages. "Arrests," he said, "Will continue until such time as the owners and drivers of machines observe the provisions of this law."

Officer Grossman and driver Harry Brown are onboard the 1907 patrol wagon, which was powered by an electric battery. According to Roderick Petersen, "Whenever a call had to be made on a hill, the horses had to be called out because [it] was incapable of pulling anywhere except on level ground."

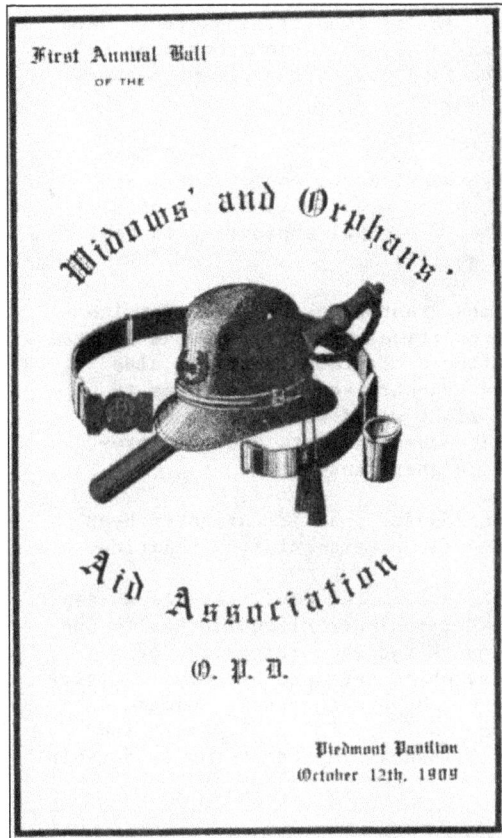

First Annual Ball
OF THE

Widows' and Orphans' Aid Association

O. P. D.

Piedmont Pavilion
October 12th, 1909

The Widows and Orphans Aid Association was founded in 1908 after Officer James Fenton was killed in the line of duty. Fenton left a wife and two children. Because, as Roderick Petersen wrote, "Collections were oftentimes very inadequate . . . the members of the department formed themselves into an association to create . . . a common fund" with which to assist survivors. Annual balls and other fund-raising activities added to it. The association continues to this day. (Courtesy of the Oakland History Room.)

EIGHTH ANNUAL BALL
benefit of the
Widows and Orphans
Aid Association
of the
Oakland Police Department

Oakland
Municipal Auditorium
Tuesday Evening
October 12, 1920

In 1907, Chief Wilson and Captain Petersen reorganized the Detective Bureau. It was renamed the Bureau of Criminal Investigation, and the detectives became inspectors, a title borrowed from Scotland Yard. In 1910, the bureau included, from left to right, (first row) H. E. Green, William Quigley, Captain Petersen, St. Clair Hodgkins, and Dennis Holland; (second row) Tim Flynn, William Kyle, Lou Agnew, Richard McSorley, James T. Drew, and Harry Caldwell. St. Clair Hodgkins was a former chief and James Drew a future one. (Courtesy of the Oakland History Room.)

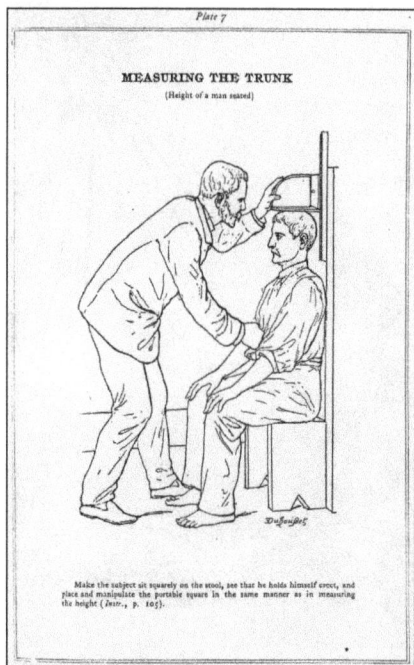

Chief Wilson obtained funds to create a Bureau of Identification, and Oakland became the first police department west of Chicago to maintain specialized criminal identification files. Initially the files included "Bertillon measurements" as well as fingerprints. Bertillionage was a method of identification developed in France and based on the use of 11 specific body measurements—the trunk, as shown; height; the reach of the arms spread horizontally; the width of the head; the length of the right ear; the diameter of the cheekbones; and the length of the left foot, the left little finger, the left forearm, the left middle finger, and the head. Within limits, this method worked, and Oakland officers used it to identify several fugitives. Eventually this cumbersome system was replaced completely by fingerprinting.

This lottery ticket was issued in Chinatown. Gambling represented a deep conflict of mores between the Chinese community and the majority population. The police and the city government eventually gave up all practical hope of ending illegal gambling, aiming instead to limit it with such means as were available—individual arrests and occasional raids. Times and people change: illegal lotteries eventually declined, a state lottery was enacted in 1984, and casinos are now legal. (Courtesy of the Oakland History Room.)

萬 夜 利 殿

MAN LEE NIGHT TIME

A Chinese Lottery Ticket with 80 Characters

This picture shows a Chinese gambling house at the beginning of the 20th century.

Trolley cars surround the Flatiron Building at San Pablo Avenue and Broadway in 1911. (Courtesy of the Oakland History Room.)

Looking east on Broadway in 1911, horses still outnumber automobiles. Though no one realized it at the time, this photograph shows the end of an era. Automoblies were about to make radical changes in urban traffic patterns. (Courtesy of the Oakland History Room.)

The Key Route Inn at Twenty-second Street and Broadway is no more, but it had a jaunty look in 1912. (Courtesy of the Oakland History Room.)

Walter J. Petersen became chief in 1912. Like Chief Wilson, Chief Petersen was a creative innovator. Along with modernizing the uniforms, he made many changes designed to improve the department's technical efficiency, including the installation of electronic semaphores to regulate downtown traffic. He introduced formal arrest reports, requiring officers to write down the events leading to an arrest, the actions they took, and the names and addresses of witnesses. One copy went to the prosecutor's office and the other to the chief before it was filed with the department's records. (Courtesy of the Oakland History Room.)

Chief Petersen increased the use of motorcycles, establishing Oakland's first Motorcycle Squad in 1914. It was equipped with 10 Indian motorcycles. (Courtesy of the Oakland History Room.)

Captain Lynch, Mayor Mott, and Chief Petersen review the department during the Annual Inspection on May 1, 1914. (Courtesy of the Oakland Police Officers Association.)

Captain Brown leads officers from East Oakland's Melrose Station in review during the Annual Inspection. (Courtesy of the OPOA.)

Police chauffeurs stand by their vehicles for inspection. When the department rented the Auto-Car, no police officer knew how to drive it, but this was soon remedied. Chauffeurs were considered to have a special skill.

Two unidentified officers pose proudly with their new 1914 Ford patrol car. From 1906 onward, the department became increasingly motorized, and in November 1917, its last four horses were sold at a city auction. (Courtesy of the Oakland History Room.)

On March 15, 1914, Chief Petersen confronted "Kelly's Army," a group of 700 to 2,000 unemployed working men who set out for Washington, D.C., to demand jobs, decent working conditions, and a living wage. The chief of the San Francisco Police Department ordered them to leave town and then telephoned Chief Petersen to let him know they were coming to Oakland. Chief Petersen requested assistance from Berkeley and Emeryville. When the marchers arrived by ferry, they were searched for weapons. They were then escorted to the Emeryville border and put on a train headed for Richmond, where the march ended in a riot. The uniformed officers are Chief Peterson, Sergeant Schroeder, and Captains Brow and Bock. (Courtesy of the Oakland History Room.)

This remarkable photograph from 1913 shows old city hall standing in front of its successor. When the new city hall opened, the old one was torn down and burned in a big, celebratory bonfire. The police department received a lot of space in the new building, including a jail on the 11th floor. (Courtesy of the Oakland History Room.)

On Independence Day, 1915, Chief Petersen and his guests ride in the department's touring car. Pictured are, from left to right, Chief Petersen, police commissioner Anderson, Berkeley chief Vollmer, Officer Eddie Hughes, and Capt. Charles Bock.

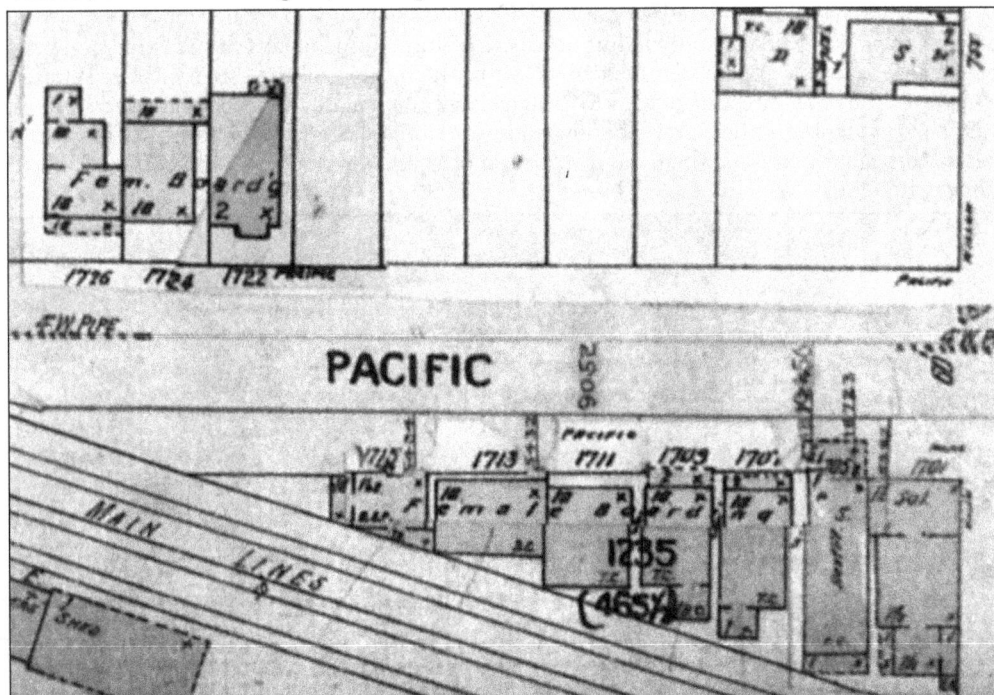

Sometime in the 1890s, Oakland joined other municipalities in tolerating "segregated districts," if they followed rules enforced by the police. As Fred Turner, the commissioner of Public Safety, put it, laws against prostitution were "held in abeyance." The Sanborn map from 1911 shows the location of "Female Boarding Houses" in West Oakland, and there were others downtown, near Sixth Street and Broadway. After the legislature passed a red-light abatement act in March 1913, the commissioner ordered Oakland's 31 brothels closed, effective midnight December 31, 1913, and the department carried out the order. (Courtesy of the Oakland History Room.)

When the United States entered World War I, Oakland's shipyards expanded rapidly, employing more than 50,000 workers and building at least 135 ships. To help prevent industrial accidents or sabotage, the department obtained a boat with which to patrol the estuary. Chief Petersen issued a special order directing officers to "watch all telegraph manholes, pipe lines, electric lines, gas plants [and] places where powder or dynamite are stored." Enormous quantities of munitions passed through the city, and there was realistic fear of a vast explosion. (Courtesy of the Oakland History Room.)

Mayor Davie makes a patriotic speech to the troops. One of Oakland's best-loved mayors, Davie was the dominant figure in Oakland politics for 15 years (1915–1930). He was a master of the commission style of governance and personally honest, but he was careless about the integrity of some of his appointees. (Courtesy of the Oakland Public Library.)

The Merchants' Exchange sponsored this street dance for soldiers at Nineteenth and Harrison Streets in 1918.

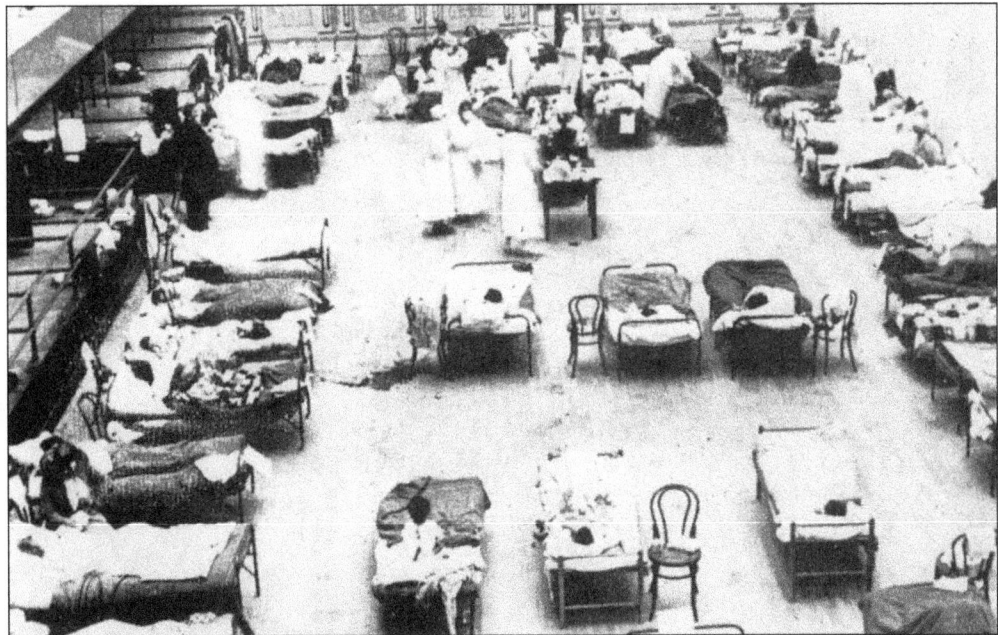

The Spanish influenza in 1918–1919 overwhelmed Oakland's medical facilities and caused more than 1,000 deaths in the area; worldwide, approximately 20 million people were killed. The pandemic reached Oakland in the late summer of 1918 and lasted into early spring of 1919. Police volunteers helped the city physician assemble the Municipal Influenza Clinic. Some of the bedridden patients in this photograph were dying. (Courtesy of the Oakland Public Library.)

On Armistice Day, November 11, 1918, everyone came downtown to celebrate the end of the war. By noontime, there was a joyful, monumental traffic jam on Broadway. Somewhere in that crowd a policeman may be trying to direct traffic. (Courtesy of the Oakland History Room.)

On April 28, 1919, the 159th Infantry returned home. A parade, held in their honor, took them by a reviewing stand in front of city hall. At least 100,000 people came to see them, and the police were busy keeping the crowd in order. Once the war was over, people wanted to throw off the moral seriousness of progressivism and the stress of patriotic ardor and enjoy themselves. They were ready for the Roaring Twenties. (Courtesy of the Oakland History Room.)

Four

BETWEEN THE WARS

The 1920s were a time of extraordinary prosperity for Oakland. The population rose during the decade from 150,000 to almost 300,000, and the number of factories increased from some 450 before the war to 1,500. Many new enterprises began, and there were wonderful civic improvements, including the construction of Lakeside Drive and the separation of Lake Merritt from the estuary. For the department, which also doubled in size, traffic enforcement was one of the major issues stemming from prosperity. Automobiles proliferated in all parts of the city. The police taught pedestrians to understand and obey traffic lights. The department's skills in crowd control were demonstrated during Charles Lindbergh's visit to the new Oakland Municipal Airport. In Prohibition enforcement, however, it had a mixed record.

When the economic collapse of 1929 enveloped the city, many hardworking people became paupers. Alameda County's welfare caseload rose by 800 percent in less than three years. For those who avoided destitution, personal income fell by 50 percent or more. City revenues fell precipitously, and new development stopped almost completely throughout the city and county. The department was not exempt; plans for the adoption of a two-way radio system were delayed for a decade, and the number of patrol cars was reduced. Social tensions increased, and the department coped with such strife-ridden events as the waterfront strike of 1934.

As the Depression deepened, federal intervention in the economy through the Works Progress Administration and other programs eased people's hardships. Skilled workers for whom there was no employment in private industry began creating lasting civic ornaments, including the Oakland Rose Garden and the Westminster Amphitheater. The most ambitious federal project was, of course, the construction of the San Francisco-Oakland Bay Bridge.

As World War II approached, the city cooperated with the federal government on essential projects for the future, such as the construction of the Oakland Army Base and the Naval Supply Center. The police department joined with the military, escorting convoys and training military policemen.

Chief J. Frank Lynch kept the department on an even keel during the graft trials of former chief Nedderman. (Nedderman was charged with taking gambling, prostitution, and bootlegging payoffs during the war but never convicted). Chief Lynch is pictured here representing Oakland at the funeral of San Francisco's Chief White in 1920. When, as a reassertion of the department's integrity, Chief Lynch directed Lt. William Woods to establish a "police school," he authorized the beginning of formal training in the department. Lynch subsequently served as captain of the Central Division until 1940. (Courtesy of the Oakland Public Library.)

In 1925, captain of inspectors Richard McSorley, pictured here, helped a young, green assistant district attorney named Earl Warren crack the "Golet Oil Company" swindle, which involved a supposed secret oil deal in Mexico. Gullible investors lost millions. It was Warren's first big case.

Sometime after the police school began, the *Tribune*'s cartoonist noticed what was happening. The classes actually taught were first aid by the Red Cross, criminal law by district attorney Decoto and judges from the police court, criminal identification by Inspector Caldwell, and traffic law by Sergeant Fahy. (Courtesy of the Oakland Public Library.)

An unidentified officer joins in the fight against a fire in Leona Heights. (Courtesy of the Oakland Public Library.)

Mayor Davie (left) and Eddie Rickenbacker, the famous World War I ace (second from left), greet the arrival of a plane carrying the first air mail to Oakland. Rickenbacker worked with Oakland officers on an unsuccessful project to develop a police air patrol. (Courtesy of the Oakland Public Library.)

Earl Warren (left) and his mentor, district attorney Ezra Decoto, are pictured here in an early 1920s photograph. DeCoto encouraged Warren to make a career in public service. Warren conducted a classic prosecution of crooked paving contractors in Oakland that caused three city commissioners to resign, sent one to prison, and led Oakland to adopt the city manager system of governance. His memoirs give an invaluable, if somewhat incomplete, picture of Oakland in the 1920s and 1930s. He went on to become district attorney of Alameda County, governor of California, and chief justice of the U.S. Supreme Court. (Courtesy of the Oakland Public Library.)

Lt. Charles Hemphill points to Oakland's first stop sign. When modern traffic signals were installed, the department enlisted the Boy Scouts to teach pedestrians the difference between red and green lights. Between 1921, when the first records were kept, and 1930, Oakland averaged 67 traffic fatalities per year.

Donald Marshall (third from the left), appointed in 1927, was one of the few chiefs from outside the department. He had served in the military police during World War I and subsequently held various positions in law enforcement. He was a detective on Earl Warren's staff at the time of his appointment. (Courtesy of the Oakland Public Library.)

The Oakland Municipal Airport was built in 1927. When Charles Lindbergh (right) flew in to inspect it, 50,000 people turned out to see him. The department received a letter of thanks from the airport superintendent for keeping the crowd orderly and off the runway. (Courtesy of the Port of Oakland.)

Early flights across the Pacific were dangerous explorations of the unknown. The first successful flight to Hawaii was made from the Oakland Municipal Airport by Lt. Albert Hegenberger and Lt. Lester Maitland in *The Bird of Paradise*, pictured here just before takeoff. (Courtesy of the Port of Oakland.)

Long-distance flying became a fad, and this led to the tragic fiasco of the Dole Hawaiian Island Derby. Of the 12 planes entered in the race from Oakland to Hawaii, only two actually got there. The day before the race, Ernie Smith (center), the pilot of the *City of Oakland*, is pictured with Jack Frost (second from left) and Gordon Scott (second from right). Frost and Scott were both lost at sea. (Courtesy of the Port of Oakland.)

After their safe return, Maitland and Hegenberger rode in triumph through downtown Oakland as newsreel camera operators and escorting police officers kept watch. (Courtesy of the Port of Oakland.)

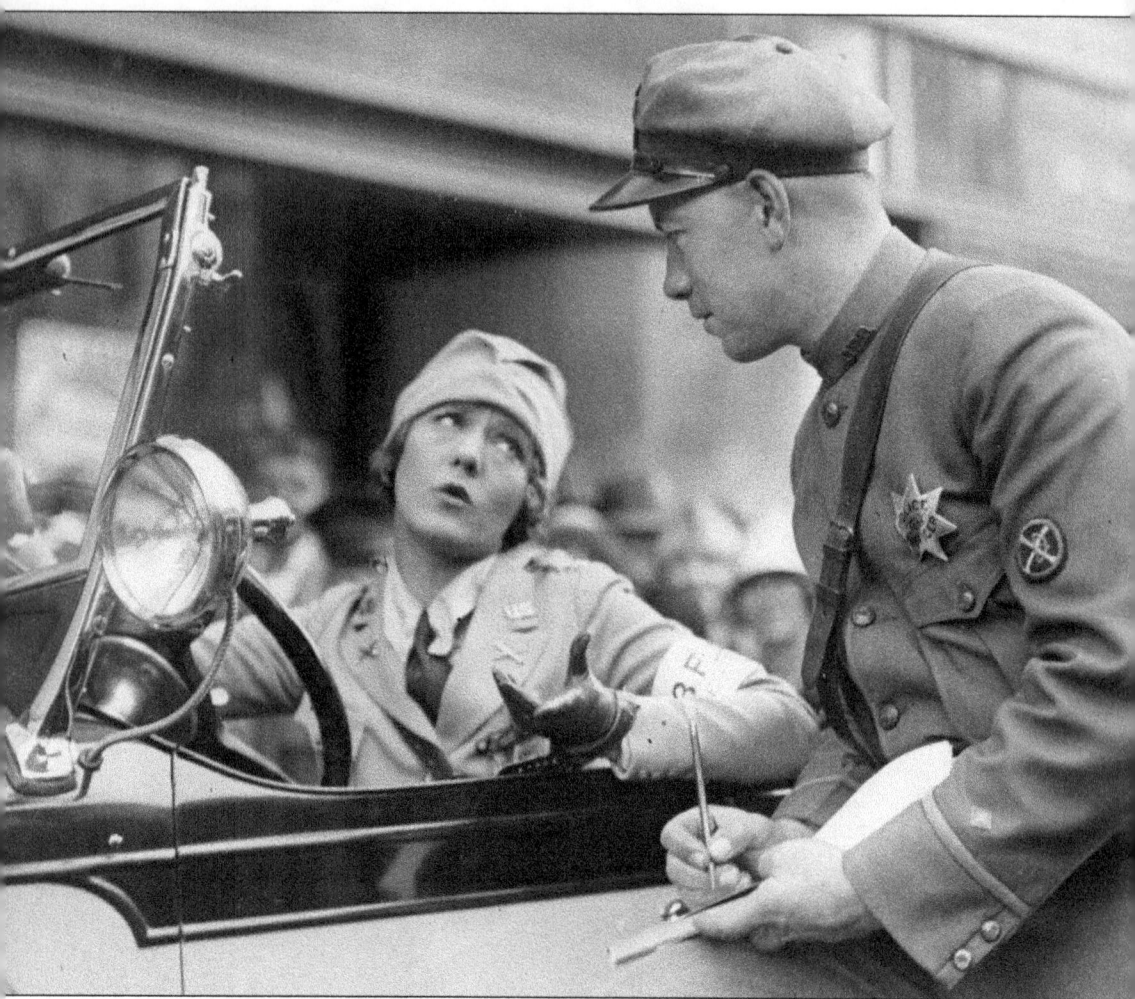

Mary Pickford and Officer "Bow Wow" Goodwin are pictured at the November 11, 1927, Armistice Parade. "Little Mary" had been an honorary member of one of the Oakland units in World War I, and she came back to Oakland for events honoring the veterans.

The Veterans Memorial Building at Grand and Harrison Streets was dedicated in October 1928.

Inspector W. J. Davis was killed in the line of duty. His funeral cortege of is seen as it leaves Sacred Heart Church at Fortieth and Grove Streets (now Fortieth Street and Martin Luther King Way) on the morning of January 7, 1928. (Courtesy of the Oakland Public Library.)

NRA MEMBER

U.S.

WE DO OUR PART

"This is the time when you and I know that though we have proceeded a portion of the way, the longer, harder part still lies ahead; and that it is for us to redouble our efforts to care for those who must still depend on relief, to prevent the disintegration of home life . . . we must be bound together by ties of neighborliness . . . the guiding spirit of our work for the sick, for the children in need, and for the aged and friendless."

PRESIDENT FRANKLIN DELANO ROOSEVELT

Depression Iconography

When the stock market crashed in 1929, the effects soon reached Oakland, and business fell off precipitously for shippers, brokers, packers, and others. Unemployment rose. City revenue declined sharply, and the police department budget was cut severely. At times, civil servants, including police officers, were paid in "script," certificates the city promised to redeem. Franklin Roosevelt carried Oakland in the 1932 presidential election as people voted for the New Deal and the NRA.

This photograph shows Inspector Walter Garrett and Officer Eddie Thompson at the scene of a homicide on Mountain Boulevard. The 1928 Chevrolet may still have the bodies inside. (Courtesy of the OPOA.)

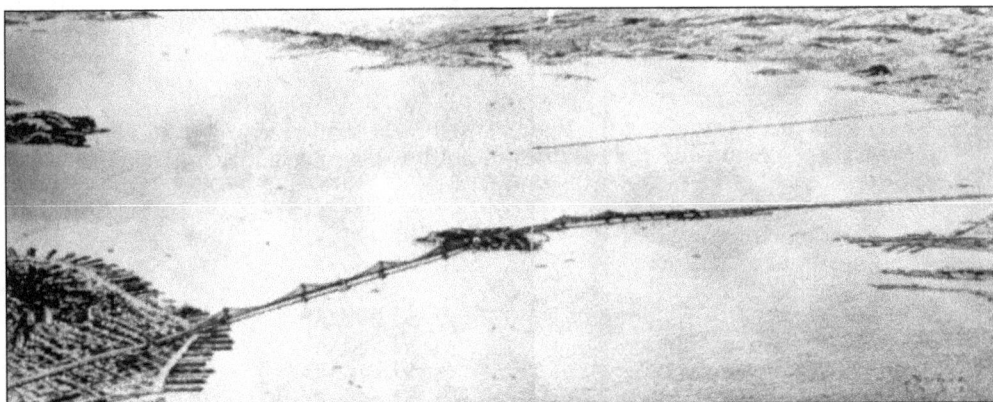

An artist's conception of the proposed San Francisco-Oakland Bay Bridge was drawn in 1933, the year work on the bridge began. It opened for use in 1936.

William J. McCracken was elected mayor in 1933 and served until 1941. He saw Oakland through the 1934 General Strike, the building of the Bay Bridge, and the lobbying effort that helped Oakland obtain the Naval Supply Center. For $1, Oakland sold the navy 500 acres of "a watery marsh on the western edge [of the city], a favorite spot for duck hunters." (Courtesy of the Oakland Public Library.)

Chief Bodie Wallman led the department through the second half of the Depression and most of World War II.

Today's Alameda County Courthouse was dedicated in October 1935. "The House That Warren Built" is located at the western end of Lake Merritt, near where Horace Carpentier's Twelfth Street Bridge had been 80 years before.

Officer Joseph Tusher survived into his 90s, becoming the oldest living retired officer before he too passed on. In his last years, he was very proud of this accomplishment but a little forgetful about his career.

Officer Ed O'Brien stands beside the ambulance assigned to the Eastern Division sometime in the 1930s.

Philena Bickell, Oakland Police Department statistician, worked with representatives of IBM to find practical applications for punch cards in police work. Her research led to the development of forms for information processing, which were adopted by many American police departments.

The German cruiser *Karlsruhe* paid a courtesy call to the Bay Area in 1935. The Oakland branch of the Steuben Society of America feted the crew, and they marched in a parade through downtown Oakland. The sailors were friendly, but according to one observer, "They said 'Heil Hitler' and made the German salute after practically every sentence." Because of the parade's political overtones, police officers were present to keep order, just as they had been when the Emergency Campaign for the Relief of German Jewry held a fund-raising event at the Oakland Auditorium.

The San Francisco-Oakland Bay Bridge is a splendid achievement by any standard. (Courtesy of the Oakland Public Library.)

Five

WORLD WAR II

Japan attacked the United States at 8:00 a.m. on December 7, 1941. By mid-morning, news flashes on the radio let people in Oakland know something awful had happened at Pearl Harbor. The department went on emergency alert. As Dexter Mast remembered, "The people who worked and lived on my beat looked to me for inside information and for instructions for their safety. I was their cop. I didn't know much more than they did from reading the newspapers, but I did represent their government as never before or since."

Oakland's contribution to the war effort was dominated by industrialist Henry J. Kaiser (1882–1967), who revolutionized the speed with which ships could be built, reducing a process that had taken months or years to a matter of days. More than a thousand ships—Liberty ships, Victory ships, and small aircraft carriers—were built in his shipyards in Oakland, Richmond, and elsewhere.

Because thousands of men in the Bay Area suddenly entered military service, an acute regional labor shortage developed. Kaiser solved this problem for his enterprises by setting up (as Beth Bagwell noted) "a mammoth recruitment division of Kaiser Industries to travel to other states. Its representatives brought some 38,000 newcomers to California." He also set up training schools for female workers. By 1944, when Kaiser's wartime employment reached 197,000, a quarter of the workers were women.

Kaiser's recruitment program helped change the size of Oakland's population and its racial composition. Thousands of people who came to work in the war industries or were stationed here in the military services decided to stay. Oakland's African American population grew from 8,462 in 1940 to 37,327 by 1945.

The same labor shortage that afflicted industry also hit public services. So many police officers went into military service that the department was shorthanded. Wartime conditions required special measures, and this led to a series of "firsts"—the use of volunteer patrol officers (mounted units) as part of civil defense, more civilian employees, and the appointment of a female and two African American officers.

Henry J. Kaiser played a leading role in Oakland's contribution to the war effort. He was not alone, however, as many companies and individuals made large contributions. His lasting monuments are the Kaiser Building on Lake Merritt and the Kaiser Permanente Hospital on MacArthur Boulevard.

In his memoirs, Dexter Mast (right) wrote, "During the first blackouts, hundreds of people roamed the streets, all quite enthusiastic about putting out lights, even if they had to heave a brick through a window . . . Friday, December 12, was a bad day. The watch started with a blackout that lasted from 7:30 to 10 p.m. Our lieutenant conducted the lineup by flashlight. . . . We were anxious to get to our beats because we knew the crowds were a little crazy. . . . There had been a rumor that forty planes had been sighted near the Golden Gate. A citizen complained that Peterson's liquor store was still open. The bars had been closed. Pete came over and asked me whether he should close or not. He seemed greatly relieved when I said I felt that he should close. We did not need drunken patriots."

72

AIR RAID RULES

AIR RAID ALARM

These are the official air raid warning signals which have been adopted for San Francisco and the eight counties bordering San Francisco Bay.

No "alert" will be sounded. Instead, a signal—designed for uniformity throughout the eight counties—will be given for immediate, simultaneous blackout.

THE BLACKOUT SIGNAL: Fluctuating siren and whistle blasts of two minutes' duration. The blackout signal will rise and fall in tone. Watch the street lights.

FOR ALL CLEAR: A continuous signal of two minutes' duration at a steady pitch. Watch the street lights.

In San Francisco, the siren blasts will be sounded by the Ferry building siren and and by all police and fire apparatus in the city and new sirens being installed.

▼ ▼ ▼

WHAT TO DO

1—Turn out all house lights if you have not blacked out your windows. Stay home. When bombs fall, lie down on the floor away from path of flying glass.

2—If you are driving, pull car into curb, turn out lights and get under cover and lie down. Avoid crowded places and stay off the streets.

3—If incendiary bombs fall on your house, cover them with dry sand. Keep sand bags in your home. If possible keep garden hose attached to a faucet. Play a FINE SPRAY ONLY on bombs. A JET or SPLASH of water will make them explode.

4—If you have a soda-and-acid extinguisher (the kind you use upside down), put your finger over nozzle to make spray. Don't use the small cylinders of liquid on bombs. They are all right for ordinary fires.

5—Under raid conditions, fill your bathtub and all buckets for Fire Department in case water mains are broken. Locate your nearest fire alarm box now and use it instead of a telephone.

6—If gas is used, go to the most inside room of your house (fewest doors and windows). Paste paper over windows, stuff cracks in doors and windows with rags.

7—Appoint one member of the house now as air raid warden to take charge and remember all the rules.

8—Above all, be calm. Stay home. The enemy wants you to create a panic and rush into the streets and highways. Don't do it. Safety lies in taking proper shelter and combating incendiary bombs correctly. Keep blacked out until the all clear.

In the early days of the war, Dexter Mast was doubtful about the value of air-raid rules and blackouts: "Actually the blackouts were, for the most part, ineffective. Most of the people on the streets carried flashlights, and many were lighting and smoking cigarettes. The glow from the cigarettes alone could mark the city's position from a long way off. Still, the blackouts were great for involving everyone in the war effort."

On May 7, 1942, five months after Pearl Harbor, Japanese Americans board buses for internment camps, as a motorcycle officer watches from the corner. There were 540 people transported from Oakland to an assembly center at Tanforan racetrack in San Bruno. From there, they were taken to camps in the interior of the country. (Fred Korematsu, an Oakland resident, was arrested and convicted for refusing to report for internment. He appealed his sentence, and it was overturned by the U.S. Supreme Court in 1983.) (Courtesy of the Oakland Public Library.)

Paul Robson, the great African American actor and singer, came to Oakland in September 1942 and led workers at the Moore Dry Dock Company in song. At this point in the war, most of the workers were still white males. (Courtesy of the Oakland Public Library.)

Men who were ineligible for military service often volunteered for other roles. This mounted unit patrolled remote areas in the hills not covered by the regular police.

The USS *War Hawk* was launched from the Moore Dry Dock Company on April 3, 1943. A freighter, it nevertheless carried gun turrets for defense against air attacks. (Courtesy of the Oakland Public Library.)

Adrien C. Bridges (above) and Leon S. Daniels were the department's first African American officers. They were appointed as emergency patrolmen ("duration officers") in July 1943 and remained with the department until 1949. They were soon joined by three more African Americans: Louis Leonard, James Whitfield, and Jim Carey. The first African American to receive a regular, non-emergency appointment was Claude Buchanan, who served 13 years. With the appointment of these officers, the department became racially integrated. During the next two decades, however, the number of African American officers increased too slowly for the department's critics. This became a matter of public controversy in the 1970s.

Kay Conway was appointed as a policewoman in 1943. She was a "duration officer" and worked as a plainclothes officer in the Vice Detail, receiving "very satisfactory" ratings. After the war, she was assigned to Juvenile and Missing Persons Details until her resignation in 1947.

Chief Robert P. Tracy (center) and Vice Mayor H. L. Beach (right) welcome Gov. Earl Warren (left) to the 1944 Widows and Orphan's Ball.

Criminalist John Davis began his long career in Oakland in 1944. A graduate of the University of California, Berkeley, where he had studied with Dr. Paul Kirk and Dr. O. W. Wilson, he earned wide recognition for his expertise in the analysis of fingerprint and firearms evidence.

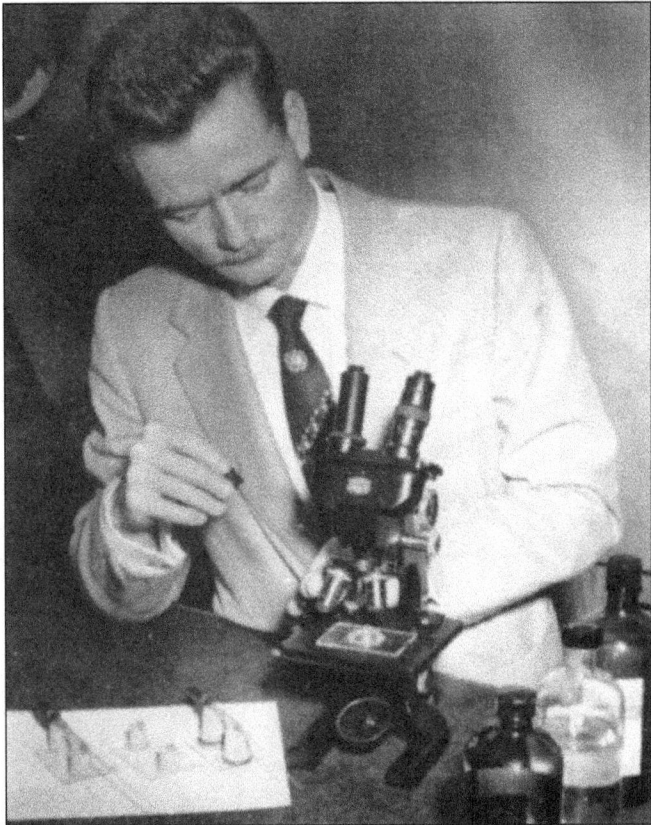

In April 1944, the Traffic Detail passed in review at Lake Merritt.

Home from the war, the cruiser USS *Oakland* is tied up at the Grove Street Pier ready to receive visitors.

Six

YEARS OF CHANGE

After World War II, the United States enjoyed a historically unprecedented burst of prosperity. With ups and downs, including the Korean War, the postwar boom lasted into the second Eisenhower administration. As had happened in earlier times, Oakland reflected life in the country at large and shared in the general well-being. New business prospered, and the city undertook the construction of new roads, parks, and schools.

At first, the unevenness in the distribution of Oakland's prosperity did not capture public attention. Industries expanded by the war now shrank, and the old industrial base atrophied. In shipbuilding, notably, area employment dropped from some 250,000 jobs to fewer than 12,000. (The Moore yards closed in 1949.) Many former workers in war industries suddenly fell into poverty, and large numbers of them belonged to minority groups.

For the police department, the opening years of the postwar era were marked by outstanding technical and professional accomplishments. It inaugurated a new Personnel and Training Division, which absorbed the old police school, and began regular recruit academies. There were advances in criminalistics and experiments with air patrol. The department's performance reached a high point in 1955 when only eight homicides and 34 deaths in traffic were reported.

In Oakland, 1955 was a pivotal year. Business had faltered, and the tax base began eroding. By 1963, the federal government declared the city a depressed area. The police department's accomplishments were obscured by an investigation of corruption that led to a major reorganization. Chiefs Divine, Vernon, and Toothman centralized the department's operations and created the Internal Affairs Section and the Planning and Research Division.

Oakland was living through major population changes that were to have important consequences. The number of people in minority groups increased continuously, rising from 5 percent in 1940 to 26 percent in 1960. The department recognized Oakland's racial divisions sooner than other branches of the city government and began conducting community relations programs in the 1940s. In 1956, as Chief Preston wrote, it "instituted a civil rights training program for all administrative and supervisory personnel, which was conducted by the Federal Bureau of Investigation."

The FBI Academy in Virginia offered excellent training to officers from all around the country. In this photograph, Oakland inspector William Brock (second from right) participates with officers from other agencies in a mock homicide investigation. He eventually rose to the rank of deputy chief.

In 1946, the department conducted an experiment with aircraft, and the pilots came to the same conclusion Oakland police pilots had reached in the 1920s—aircraft could not patrol urban areas efficiently. Even so, they made useful mercy flights, delivering medical supplies to remote towns as far away as Montana. In this informal photograph are, from left to right, (first row, kneeling) officers Howard Fellows, Harry Jones, Thomas Turner, Robert Phillips, and Fred Marshall; (second row, standing) Sgt. Edmund Thompson; Officers Martin Nissen, Gene Engstrom, Victor Lagerson, and William Marshall; and Sgt. Eddie Ray.

This photograph shows weapons training at the postwar academy. Many recruits had been members of the armed forces, and it seemed natural to adopt uniforms cut in a military style.

An instructor teaches trainees how to ride motorcycles on wet sand. They learned to start, stop, and abandon their bikes in conditions simulating what they would encounter on wet streets in stormy weather.

This appears to be traffic school for people cited for "driving under the influence." "Sec 510," written on the chalkboard, was formerly the vehicle code section for DUI.

The Radio Room was in Central Division on the first floor of city hall. The operator in this late-1940s photograph is not identified.

These photographs show patrol cars from the late 1940s and early 1950s, when the department began using black and whites.

Here a teletype operator prepares to send a message. These machines were once vital for rapidly providing information to many agencies simultaneously. A sort of proto-internet, they helped the department apprehend fleeing suspects in distant places (as, for example, in the murder of Oakland officer Kohler, when the killers were located in a small town in Utah).

With the passage of time, the volume of records kept by the department increased steadily, and the department depended on non-sworn employees to maintain them. Statisticians are pictured here processing reports and other information. (Courtesy of the OPOA.)

Watchmen, how goes the night? Pictured here are motor officers working the graveyard shift in the 1950s.

The championship Motorcycle Drill Team displays its skills at a Veterans Day Parade in 1954.

This photograph shows Chief Lester J. Divine (back row, fourth from left) with California Highway Patrol officers at the University of California, Berkeley. (His successor, Capt. Wyman Vernon, is at the far left in the back row.) In his thesis at Northwestern University, Divine sketched visionary plans for the department. On becoming chief in 1949, he restored the rank of policewoman, began issuing departmental publications to all officers, and initiated programs devoted to racial issues. Answering charges of biased law enforcement, he said, "I want impartial law enforcement . . . I believe that at all times the police department must be scrupulously honest with the public it serves." He recognized, as James Q. Wilson later wrote, that Oakland had become "a racially divided city" and that police work had "large policy implications." (Courtesy of the OPOA.)

Joseph R. Knowland Sr., the editor and publisher of the *Oakland Tribune* from 1915 to 1966, had enormous influence in Oakland. When relations between city manager Wayne Thompson and Chief Divine broke down, Knowland acted as intermediary in the discussions, which led to Divine's resignation in 1955.

Chief Vernon is pictured inspecting the motorcycle unit. During his administration, the department closed the Northern and Eastern stations and concentrated operations in headquarters downtown. In *Varieties of Police Experience*, James Q. Wilson described the department (under the name Westville) as having a "legalistic" style, meaning that it put great emphasis on strict interpretation of the law. (Courtesy of the OPD.)

City manager Wayne Thompson authorized a new police headquarters at Seventh Street and Broadway as part of a plan to revitalize Oakland's skid row, and it became a major project for the Planning and Research Division. Sgt. Charles Gain, left, and Officer Jim Linzen are pictured at work on plans for the new building. (Courtesy of the OPD.)

An architect's model of the projected headquarters (pictured on the cover of a Training Section publication) presented a design featuring a relatively open and welcoming lobby with great glass windows to let in natural light. This was changed after several bombings in the 1960s.

TRAINING UPDATE

February, 1988   Vol. 8, No. 1

An officer throws a smoke bomb through an open window while others provide cover during the "Essex Street Siege" in North Oakland. The officers are unidentified.

Chief Toothman presents an award to policewoman Mary Hilliard. She was the last policewoman to remain on active service after the rank was phased out in the 1970s.

The Oakland skyline is seen here in the 1960s when (except for the Police Administration Building) there were no high-rise buildings below Fourteenth Street, and the city had been designated a depressed area.

The Police Administration Building opened in 1962. Over the years, it has validated city manager Wayne Thompson's vision by playing an important part in making "Old Oakland" possible and bringing people into the area between Seventh and Tenth Streets, where visitors now find attractive restaurants and art galleries.

Seven

THE VIETNAM ERA

Many people look back on the 1960s with nostalgia, which is surprising because it was an unhappy time in so many ways. Nationally, the murders of Pres. John F. Kennedy, his brother Robert, and the Reverend Martin Luther King were signature events. Roiling quarrels over civil rights and Vietnam spread across the country dividing regions, states, communities, and families. Oakland was deeply affected by national issues.

Locally, the Vietnam era began with protests at the University of California, Berkeley. When university officials attempted to regulate student political activity, student activists formed the Free Speech Movement and staged a spectacular "occupation" of a campus administration building. Protests quickly expanded beyond campus issues to center on universal student concerns, the Vietnam War and the draft. Whenever illegal assemblies got out of hand, the Berkeley Police Department invoked its mutual-aid agreements, and the Oakland Police Department honored its commitments.

Two notable antiwar demonstrations occurred in Oakland. On October 15, 1965, eight thousand protesters marched down Telegraph Avenue, intent on picketing the Oakland Army Base. They did not have an Oakland parade permit, and the department stopped them at the city line—Telegraph Avenue and Prince Street. The second demonstration, a much larger affair, was "Stop the Draft Week," held from October 16 through October 21, 1967. This involved an attempt to close the Armed Forces Induction Center at Fifteenth and Clay Streets.

The growth of Oakland's minority populations continued, and by 1970, the African American, Hispanic, and Asian communities had become the majority. This was reflected in local politics. Oakland, a Republican bastion since the 1860s, began electing Democrats, sending a stream of liberal representatives to Sacramento and Washington. Victories by such African American leaders as Lionel Wilson and Ron Dellums showed the depth of the change. They brought minority concerns to the center of Oakland politics. In the same years, the Black Panthers presented themselves as revolutionary spokespeople for black power.

In 1966, Chief Toothman retired, complaining of exhaustion, and was succeeded by Robert J. Preston (above). In addition to the unrest associated with the Vietnam War, Chief Preston found that racial conflict had increased. He believed many problems could be resolved through person-to-person contact and put this into action in 1966, when delinquent gangs committed vandalism downtown. He led a series of behind-the-scenes meetings in which he listened to complaints about the police and lack of jobs and answered questions honestly.

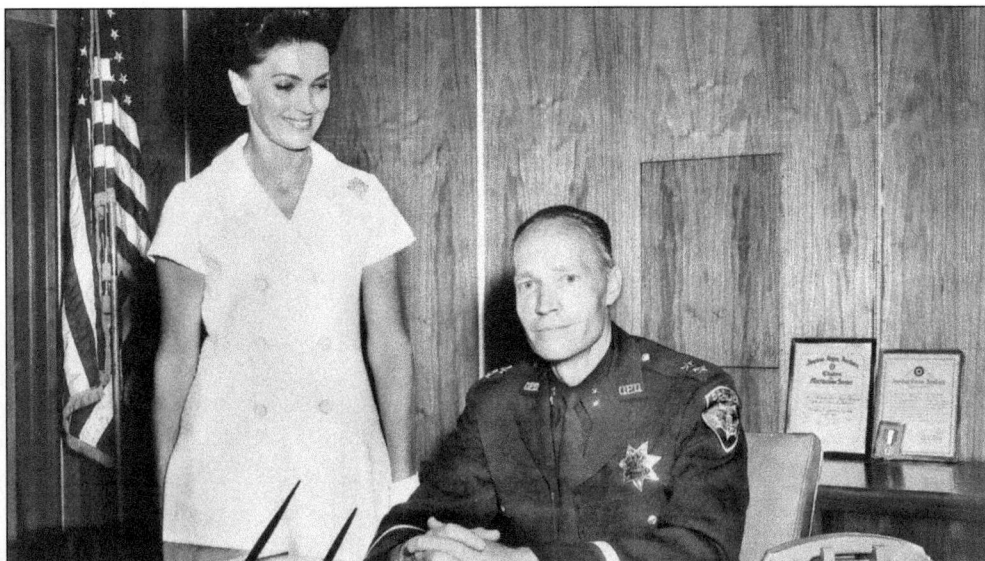

Chief Charles Gain led the department from 1967 to 1973. According to James Q. Wilson, Gain changed Oakland from a "legalistic" to a "service" department—one attaching major importance to contact with all elements of the community while keeping the peace and enforcing the law. He recognized that the city's increasing diversity required far-reaching changes in policy. Many longtime observers of Oakland believe Gain's initiatives helped save Oakland from burning when a contagion of riots swept the nation's cities. He was as unyielding toward antiwar demonstrations as Toothman or Preston.

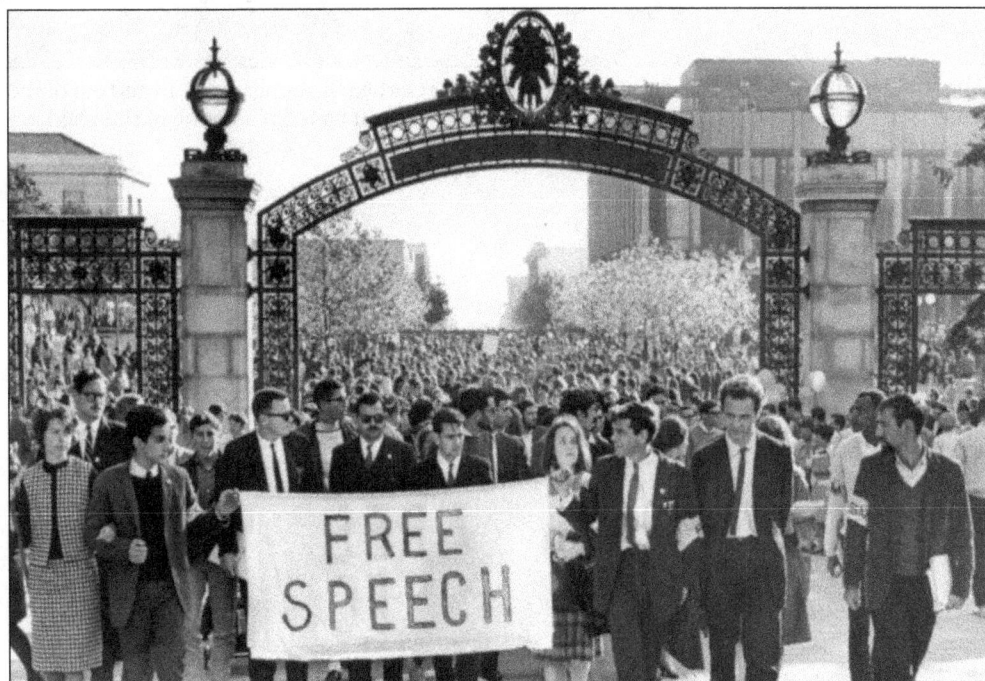

Policing the disturbances resulting from the 1964 Free Speech Movement in Berkeley became a burden for the Bay Area law enforcement community. (Courtesy of the Oakland Museum of California.)

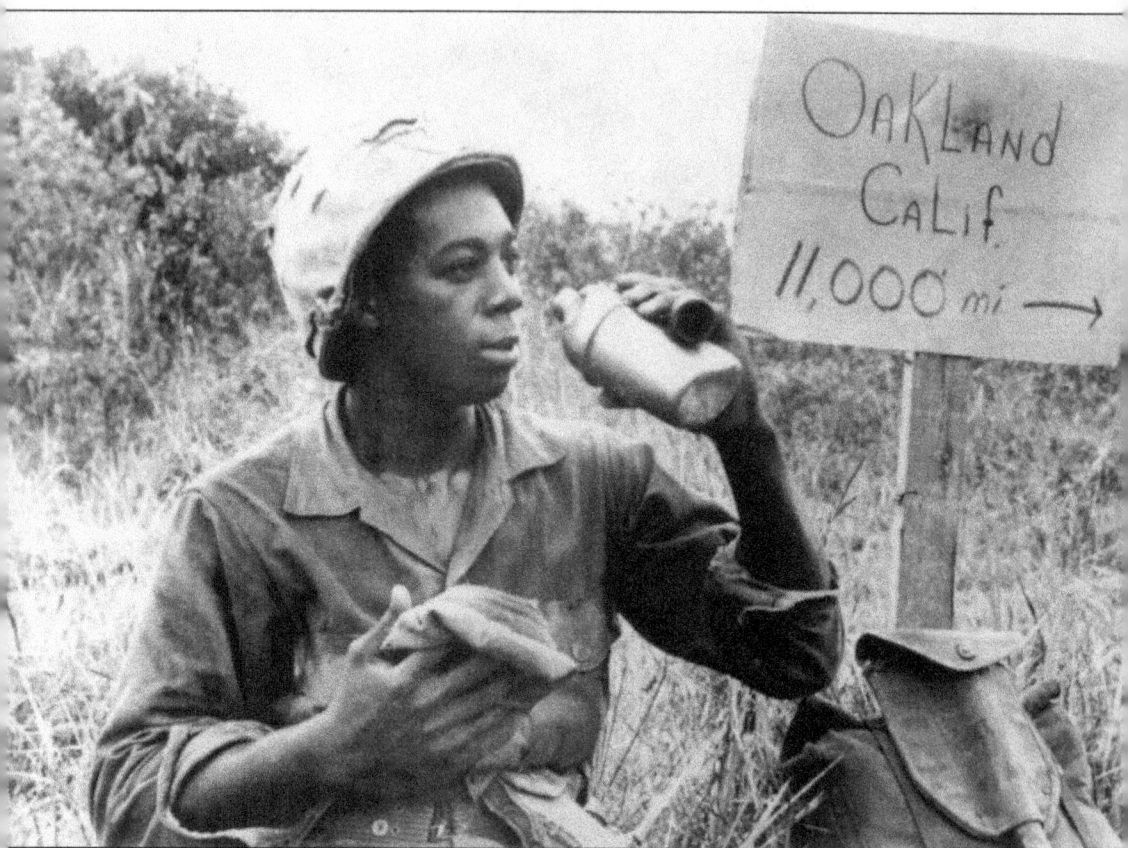

The Vietnam War, which lasted from 1964 to 1977, was loathed by young people in and out of the nation's universities. In Berkeley, it became the major student cause. (Courtesy of the Oakland Museum of California.)

Oakland was a major embarkation point for soldiers en route to Vietnam, and these soldiers are preparing to board ship in 1965. Students rowed boats into the estuary to delay the transports, picketed, and tried to stop troop trains in Berkeley by blocking the railroad tracks. (Courtesy of the Oakland Museum of California.)

At the beginning of "Stop the Draft Week" in 1967, both the protesters and police behaved fairly well. Here a demonstrator, who has gone limp, is about to be put in the wagon with other students for transportation to the county jail at Santa Rita. (Courtesy of the Oakland Museum of California.)

A FILM BY GEORGE PAUL CSICSERY

THE THURSDAY CLUB

HOW THE OAKLAND POLICE SAW THE 1960s

The tone of "Stop the Draft Week" changed quickly though. The protest became excessively violent, and there were retaliatory lapses in police discipline, including attacks on the press. Here, in a photograph sent around the nation, George Csicsery falls to the ground after being struck by an unidentified officer. Years later, Csicsery produced *The Thursday Club*, a film based on his attempt to find the officer who hit him. In the film, he interviewed a group of Oakland officers who were at that demonstration as well as one of the student leaders who helped organize it. The film also profiles two African American officers of the time, Hadwick Thompson and Booker Ealy. (Courtesy of George Csicsery.)

Hadwick Thompson had survived the battle at Pearl Harbor. After the war, he became a member of the department and served with distinction throughout the postwar years and the troubles of the 1960s. His daughter was a student at the University of California when protests were at their height. He used to drive her to school every day, dropping her off a few blocks from the campus so that students would not see her emerging from a police car. They followed this routine even when they knew he would return later for crowd-control duty at a demonstration. (Courtesy of George Csicsery.)

Many former members of the Black Panther Party have written apologias. Dissenting views are given in Hugh Pearson's *The Shadow of the Panther*, which examines the party's aura of criminality, and *For the People*, the memoirs of district attorney J. Frank Coakley. The Panthers and the student movement popularized "pig" as a term of abuse for police officers, but many officers took it in stride. One put a hat on a young pig that looked as innocent and trusting as Babe and photographed it in the front seat of a tan and white. A contest to caption the picture followed, and the winner was, "Gee, Sarge, do you mean I've passed probation?"

Eight

AND AFTERWARDS

Oakland has nurtured the economic recovery that began in the early 1970s. Two beautiful federal office buildings and modern high-rise offices have added vitality downtown. On the waterfront, Jack London Square has been enhanced by the ferry terminal, a new Amtrak station, and new stores, clubs, and restaurants that harmonize with the environment. North Oakland's Rockridge has become a fashionable locale for restaurants, coffee shops, and bookstores. Chinatown and the Fruitvale are doing well and expanding, and East Oakland has successfully wooed "big box" retail outlets along Interstate 880. There was an economic pause during the dot-com bust, but new housing has had a positive impact and private business has added thousands of new jobs to the economy.

The city was damaged by the devastating Loma Prieta earthquake on October 17, 1989 (which was especially hard on West Oakland), and the frightful wildfire in the hills two years later in October 1991. Some Oakland residents began to joke nervously about October as a time for disaster. But the losses from each setback have been made good, and Oakland's population has begun to grow again. As of this writing, approximately 400,000 people live in the city.

The election of Lionel Wilson as mayor in 1977 completed Oakland's transformation from a Republican stronghold into a Democratic bulwark. It demonstrated the power of multiracial alliances in local politics. His successors have based their governance on mediating between the needs of Oakland's different communities.

In the 1970s, the police department carried out an affirmative action program, which raised the number of female and minority officers, resulting in a department that fully reflects the diversity of the city. The department took advantage of new developments in communications and criminalistics and developed an early form of community policing. During the earthquake and fire, the department showed itself to be an agile, dedicated, and resourceful organization.

Chief George Hart led the department for 21 years (1973–1994). By the time he retired, most of the officers and employees had never worked for any other chief. He maintained a generally low public profile, and his policies aimed at reducing the potential for interpersonal conflict. He demanded that officers "accomplish the police mission as efficiently and unobtrusively as possible, with the highest regard for the human dignity . . . and with minimal reliance on the use of force and authority." His "Beat Health" program preceded "community policing" by a decade. (Courtesy of the OPOA.)

In 1974, Oakland had a minority population of slightly more than 50 percent, and the department had a minority complement of 12 percent. To end the controversy caused by this statistical disparity, the department entered into the Penn-Stump Consent Decree. The resulting affirmative action program was supervised by Chief Hart, Deputy Chief Odell Sylvester (right), and Capt. James MacArthur. The program included all of Oakland's minority groups and had special provisions for recruitment of female officers. (Courtesy of the OPD.)

In 1975, the rank of policewoman was closed to further appointments, resolving an issue the department had handled inconsistently for 60 years. In 1913, Chief Petersen appointed two policewomen, Beatrice McCall and Alice Richardson, but they were terminated in 1919 by Mayor Davie. Chief Wallman appointed Kay Conway in 1943, but Chief Tracy abolished her job in 1946. Chief Divine restored the rank in 1949 and appointed new policewomen. With the appointment of Susan Hoffman, pictured here, the department settled on a permanent policy— all females appointed to the department would be regular officers. (Courtesy of the OPD.)

The department's search for a suitable patrol aircraft ended when it discovered the helicopter. This photograph shows why—Oakland officers and FBI agents (and a television cameraman) hunt a bank robber as Argus hovers overhead. The helicopter crew easily spotted the robber hiding in the reeds.

The computer changed policing on the street in 1974 when "Digicoms" were installed in patrol cars and made all sorts of information instantly available to patrol officers. This equipment has steadily improved.

With computers, the Radio Room became the Communications Center. Dispatchers now perform specialized work that is far more complicated and stressful than what they did in the old days of telephones, teletypes, and AM radio broadcasts.

This photograph shows driver training underway on the huge parking lot of the coliseum in East Oakland. The rookies are doing well; only two traffic cones have been knocked over.

Fulfilling plans made a decade earlier, the Port of Oakland was the first on the West Coast to adapt fully to containerization, an extraordinary innovation in how freight is handled on cargo ships. The port has its own security force, but when a body arrived in a container from Japan, the investigation was turned over to the Police Homicide Detail.

The Paramount Theater, refurbished as a home for the Oakland Symphony, became the downtown venue for a wide range of entertainments, including shows put on by the Oakland Police Officers Association to raise funds for its charities.

The author is seen at work around 1976. Pictured are, from left to right, Officer Earl Halloman, the author's colleague Bob Middleton, Sgt. Leroy Sargent, Officer Larry Newman, and the author.

Bob Middleton caught Officer Fred Peoples by surprise, and Officer Jim Parr plugged his ears as a bemused recruit watches.

The morning's assignment was to take photographs for a training bulletin on felony car stops. This one shows Officer Fred Peoples, shotgun at the ready (but not cocked), crouched in a patrol car offset at an angle from "suspect" Middleton's vehicle. The engine block provides him with some protection from gunfire, and the open door obstructs the suspect's view. In a real car stop, this would give Officer Peoples a clear view of the suspect and a physical and psychological advantage. (If he had actually been driving this car, he wouldn't have had the baton in his belt. Somehow that detail was missed in this photograph.)

Mayor Lionel Wilson and César Chávez meet in Oakland. Before entering politics, Wilson had a successful legal career. He served as mayor for 14 years (1977–1991), and his administration was notable for opening employment to minorities. It also dealt with major problems in the public schools, a rising crime rate, and the aftermath of the Loma Prieta earthquake. (Courtesy of African Museum and Library at Oakland [AAMLO].)

Mounted officers Ken Douglas and Larry Davis patrol Jack London Village.

During the past 30 years, the department has made thousands of arrests for narcotics violations. One concomitant of illegal drug activity is homicide. In this case, a drug deal went bad, and this victim and her brother were murdered in their own home. Drug dealing has led to a hideous rise in Oakland's homicide rate. (Courtesy of Rick Ealy, OPD retired.)

Here Officer Pete Pruitt helps Sgt. Leroy Sargent calm down. Sergeant Sargent, unarmed, prevented a murder outside the Police Administration Building and arrested the perpetrator.

As of this writing, 48 Oakland officers have been killed in the line of duty. Chief Fenton Thompson created the department's first memorial in 1919, a flag with nine stars—one for each officer lost up to that time. Subsequently the badges of slain officers were displayed in a glass case at headquarters. Many members of the department felt this was inadequate, and in 1984, Lt. John Regan and Officer George Edwards persuaded Chief Hart to authorize a permanent memorial in the lobby of the Police Administration Building. Sgt. Tony Morgan joined the project, doing research on the details of each fatal incident.

Mike Soto, a friend of the author, is listed on the wall, as are two officers who attended the author's class on departmental history.

The Loma Prieta earthquake on October 17, 1989, registered 6.9 on the Richter scale and did enormous damage throughout Northern California. Parts of the Bay Bridge collapsed, hundreds of buildings were destroyed, and thousands more suffered major structural damage. It killed 67 people and injured at least 2,800. Its impact in Oakland surpassed that of both 19th-century quakes. A mile and a quarter of the upper lanes of the Cypress Freeway in West Oakland collapsed, pancaking onto the lower level. The department's emergency operations lasted 10 days.

This is a different section of the freeway as it looked several days after the earthquake.

According to a clerk at Mi Rancho, a market that used to be across the street from the police department, "The quake did not bother me until I looked outside and saw the top of the police building teetering over me. Then I got nervous." Parts of the building ruptured along the architectural "seams." When aftershocks rattled the upper floors, it sounded to people inside as though a freight train was rumbling through the basement. The city dithered for a few years before finally repairing the internal damage. As seen at right, the building looks to be as good as new.

The Federal Towers and City Center have added to the economic recovery of the downtown area. Downtown's revival would not have been a success without the synergistic police patrols directed by Capt. Peter Sarna. The methods applied by Sarna and his colleagues are described in *Policing A City's Central District: The Oakland Story* by Albert J. Reiss.

The Oakland Hills fire on October 19 and 20, 1991, killed 25 people, injured 150 (mostly with severe burns), and destroyed more than 3,000 homes, apartments, and condominiums. It began at about 10:30 a.m. on a windy Sunday and quickly became a firestorm. Thirteen officers responded initially; by 3:00 p.m., more than 200 officers were at the scene. This panoramic view, partly obscured by smoke, shows a small portion of the damage.

The burned-out police car in the foreground of this photograph was driven by Officer John Grubensky. He directed traffic at an intersection in the hills, guiding vehicles away from the fire. Despite the intense smoke and heat, he rescued at least 20 disoriented people. He lost his own life when he lingered too long in an attempt to save five more. As Capt. Steve Jensen said in a eulogy, "He did not shrink from danger." The department's Board of Review, directed by Deputy Chief Thomas Donohue, recorded many other acts of heroism.

After the fire, the Oakland Hills were desolate. Officer Tim Sanchez looks out over the ruin of so many hopes.

Joseph Samuels Jr., the first African American to lead the department, was sworn in on August 9, 1993. He adopted community policing as the keystone of his administration. In summarizing his term, one of his associates said, "His administration was a success because he made himself available to the community. In his dealings with people he was always fair to high and low alike. His policies definitely improved our relations with the community."

Hey! Pictured here is Officer R. E. Williams on patrol at the City Center.

For many years, the Communications Section was on the seventh floor of the Police Administration Building. It functioned without interruption during the Loma Prieta earthquake, but a decision was made to move it to a less vulnerable location. On June 25, 1999, during the dedication of the new Communications Center, senior dispatcher Phyllis Bruening is seen in conversation with retired Deputy Chief John Ream.

Here is beautiful Lake Merritt today, still a jewel in the city's crown. Somehow, the proximity of the monumental Kaiser building (in the center of the photograph) does not detract from its serenity.

Since 1975, the estuary has been patrolled by a police boat (pictured above) donated by the U.S. Coast Guard. Sgt. Gary Tolleson described it as "small enough to be maneuverable in private harbors but robust enough for emergency towing, rescue, firefighting, or pumping out a craft that has taken on water."

Sgt. Sharon Banks and criminalist Lancing Lee search a database as they work on a problem.

City hall was closed for more than a year due to earthquake damage. It was restored and refurbished with help from then-congressman Ron Dellums.

Before he was elected mayor in 1998, former governor Jerry Brown lived near the waterfront in "The Compound," the remodeled warehouse pictured here. After taking office, he obtained changes in the city charter, which made him a "strong" mayor, substantially ending the city-manager system adopted as a reform seven decades years earlier after Earl Warren's prosecution of city commissioners.

The inauguration of Chief Richard Word on July 2, 1999, was an elaborate and colorful municipal ceremony. Chief Word is pictured taking the oath of office from Mayor Brown.

Since its establishment in 1955, the Oakland Police Officers Association has represented the officers in their negotiations with city management and played an important part in their social and charitable activities. For many years, the OPOA offices were on Washington Street, a few doors away from the Police Administration Building. Its new headquarters on Fifth Street opened in 2001.

Chief Wayne Tucker succeeded Richard Word in 2005. Oakland's 45th chief, he commands a force that includes 3 deputy chiefs, 10 captains, 25 lieutenants, 136 sergeants, and 628 officers. Understaffed even at full complement, the department was short 100 officers in 2006.

Former congressman Ron Dellums is pictured at Laney College on October 7, 2005, the day he announced his candidacy for mayor. He waged a vigorous campaign to succeed Jerry Brown (who was running for the office of attorney general). With his inauguration as its 45th mayor, Oakland opened a new chapter in its civic life. (Courtesy of Michael Howerton, *Berkeley Daily Planet*.)

Oakland is pictured here as it is today, looking east from Broadway and the Embarcadero toward downtown and the hills. If Marshall McCann and his two deputies could be transported through time from 1853 to the present, they would be astonished by how the town has changed.

Nine

LIFE ON THE BEAT

Law enforcement has a lighter side. Police officers are some of the world's best storytellers, and the Alameda County District Attorney's office publishes a page of their "war stories" in each issue of *Point of View*, its excellent legal review. Stories are contributed by officers throughout the county, but these are all from Oakland officers:

A man was burglarizing a home in Oakland when he found a new pair of expensive jeans in a bag from the Gap. He also spotted a receipt in the bag. So, after finishing his work, he took the jeans and receipt to the local Gap store to get a refund. The salesman looked at the receipt and said he would have to check with his manager. A few minutes later, OPD officers arrived and arrested the burglar. As he was being escorted out in handcuffs, he yelled at the salesman, "Why'd you call the cops?" He replied, "You jerk, those jeans belong to *me*! That's *my* name and address on the receipt!" At a loss for words, the burglar said, "You've sure got a nice house."

Walnut Creek and Oakland narcotic officers were serving a search warrant on a house in Oakland where marijuana was being sold. While the search was underway, a young woman approached two officers who were standing just outside the house. "Hey, can you guys sell me some weed?" she asked. The officers were somewhat surprised because they were wearing raid jackets and their guns and handcuffs were in plain view. Just then, the woman noticed the police gear and asked, "Hey, you're not cops are you?" "No," said one of the officers, "We're going to a Halloween party *dressed* as cops." "A Halloween party in *August*?" the woman exclaimed, "That's so cool. So where's my weed?"

Dispatcher to officer: "3 L 19. A man says there's a car parked on his front lawn. It's been there for about four months and he's starting to get suspicious."

An Oakland officer who had just chased down and arrested a drug dealer asked him, "Do you know about the Three Strikes law?" The man responded, "No, man, I ain't got time for baseball. I'm too busy sellin' drugs."

An OPD officer was driving on Interstate 880 en route to his beat when a car passed him doing at least 80. When the officer stopped the car the driver screamed, "You can't write me a ticket! Only the CHP can write tickets on the freeway!" The officer, having heard this before, deadpanned, "Gee, I didn't know that. But I'm gonna write you up anyway because I'm under the quota." "Well I'm just gonna tear it up," said the driver. "You're just too smart for me," said the officer.

A man who robbed the Bank of America branch on Shattuck Avenue in Berkeley did just about everything wrong. Let us count the ways:
(1) Wrong color: For his getaway car, he stole a "passionate pink" Isuzu which naturally caught the attention of an Oakland officer as the officer was listening to a description of the getaway car on his radio.
(2) Mistaking a parking lot for the Bay: While being chased across the Bay Bridge by said officer, the robber attempted to toss his gun into the Bay. But it landed in a parking lot near the shoreline at the feet of a citizen who immediately reported it to the police.
(3) Wrong escape route: As the robber was being chased through the streets of San Francisco, he headed into the Financial District where, because of street repairs, he encountered a major traffic jam. He decided to bail.
(4) Bad aim: While being chased, he tossed his holdup note which, as if by magic, landed in the hands of one of the pursuing officers.
(5) Fumbling the money: As he continued to run, he collided with a fire hydrant. This caused him to drop the bag containing the stolen money.
(6) Losing sight of the immediate objective: He decided to stop and pick up the bag even though the pursuing officers were only 10 feet behind him. He was immediately arrested.

A murder suspect who was being questioned by homicide investigators admitted that he'd fired the shot that killed the victim, but said he was just trying to scare him. The suspect explained, "I was aiming about a foot away from him, you dig? But when the dude heard the gun go off he jumped—he jumped right in front of my bullet! So I guess you could say the dude kinda killed himself." (The jury's verdict: "Kinda guilty.")

During jury selection in a drug trial, a prospective juror said he knew the defendant. "Actually, I don't really know him," he explained, "I just see him around my neighborhood every day, you know, selling drugs to the kids." "Despite that," asked the DA, "I'm sure you can still be a fair and impartial juror, can't you?" "Of course," he replied.

Late one night on Webster Street, a robber with a handgun walked up to a man who was about to use an ATM. "Unless you wanna get shot, withdraw $200 and hand it over," said the robber. "But I don't have $200 in my account," said the man, "And I can prove it." He handed the robber his latest bank statement which showed a balance of $14. After studying the statement, the robber handed it back and walked away saying, "Man, you should be robbin' me."

BIBLIOGRAPHY

Bagwell, Beth. *Oakland: The Story of a City*. Novato, CA: Presidio Press, 1982.

Bowman, J. N. *The Peraltas and Their Houses*. Alameda, CA: Alameda County Historical Society, 2001.

Coakley, J. Frank. *For the People*. Orinda, CA: Western Star Press, 1992.

Conmy, Peter Thomas. *The Beginnings of Oakland, California*. Oakland, CA: Oakland Public Library.

Crouchett, L. P., L. G. Bunch, and M. K. Winnacker. *Visions Toward Tomorrow: The History of the East Bay Afro-American Community, 1852–1977*. Oakland, CA: Northern California Center for Afro-American History and Life, 1989.

Cummings, G. A., and E. S. Pladwell. *Oakland . . . A History*. Oakland, CA: Grant D. Miller Mortuaries, Inc., 1942.

Fibel, Peral Randolph. *The Peraltas: Spanish Pioneers and the First Family of the East Bay*. Oakland, CA: Peralta Hospital, 1958.

Mast, Dexter. *Six Gold Stars* (Vol. 1 and 2). Berkeley, CA: Glenn Press, 1990.

Muir, William. *The Police: Street Corner Politicians*. Chicago: University of Chicago, 1977.

Pearson, Hugh. *The Shadow of the Panther*. New York: Addison-Wesley, 1994.

Rather, Lois. *Oakland's Image: A History of Oakland, California*. Oakland, CA: The Rather Press, 1972.

Reiss, Albert J. *Policing A City's Central District: The Oakland Story*. Washington, D.C.: National Institute of Justice, 1985.

Skolnick, Jerome. *The New Blue Line: Police Innovation in Six American Cities*. New York: Free Press, 1986.

Wasserman, Abbey, ed. *The Spirit of Oakland*. Heritage Media Corporation, Carlsbad, CA, 2000.

Wilson, James Q. *Varieties of Police Experience*. Cambridge, MA: Harvard University Press, 1968.

Visit us at
arcadiapublishing.com

www.ingramcontent.com/pod-product-compliance
Lightning Source LLC
Chambersburg PA
CBHW050709110426
42813CB00007B/2131